A Winds

Also by Kathleen Fernandes and published by Ginninderra Press
Wicked and Whimsical

Kathleen Fernandes

A Windswept Path

Acknowledgements

Most of these poems have appeared in *Centoria, Four W, Five Bells, Polestar, Studio, The Mozzie, Fresh* and *Nineteen-O-Splash* in New Zealand, *Beyond the Rainbow, Positive Words, The Write Angle, Poetry Matters, tamba, Freexpression, Short & Twisted, The Guardian Newspaper, Oxygen,* the Women Writer's Network anthologies and *Class Act* Wednesday Night Poets anthology. 'Sameness' and 'Disconnect' were highly commended in 2004 in the St George Eisteddfod Inc Poetry Competition.

I would like to thank Norm Neill
and members of the Wednesday Night Poets
for their critique and support

A Windswept Path
ISBN 978 1 76109 312 8
Copyright © text Kathleen Fernandes 2022
Cover photo from Pexels

First published 2022 by
GINNINDERRA PRESS
PO Box 3461 Port Adelaide 5015
www.ginninderrapress.com.au

Contents

Antipathies

Making beds,
smell of garlic,
taste of vegemite,
circuses,
sarcasm,
stories without depth, clarity,
railway stations at night,
cockroaches
and people who shove
shopping trolleys
into my back.

From My Window

Shivery again.
I huddle inside my dressing gown;
reflection, obscurity.
Throat raw. Forehead fiery.
Pick up my book, return to
families who hoard secrets.
Kidnap, murder,
in Derry, Ireland.

I hear voices, sit up, peer out,
suit strides past. Across the road,
woman in tights, jogs. Suit whistles.
Her ponytail swings.
Close my book. Switch on the radio.

> *Investigations continue into the*
> *disappearance of a Saudi journalist.*
> *Then onto the Wentworth by-election.*

I lower the sound.
Notice two men,
who stare at my house. The taller one points
to my side gate, mutters to his mate.
What are they up to? Had I locked the gate?
I yawn, eyelids languish,
lean into my pillow. In seconds, they are gone.
White van screeches,
shaggy-haired figure in a clown mask, hops out.
Nearby, a young couple smoke, loiter, bicker.
Teenager in odd shoes, roars past on his skateboard.
Car doors slam. 'Daddy, Daddy.'
Next door's boys home from school.

Young couple hurl insults
at each other.
Figure in clown mask
looks on.

Straighten my pyjama jacket.
Grunt, punch my pillow.
Open my book,
return to Derry.

Red Country

Infinite.
Arid.
Furtive.

From the train,
a passenger points,
'Look at the goats, kangaroos, emus.'
A toddler, his nose smudged against
the window, giggles.

In the tree cemetery,
on Menindee Lakes,
hags, some five hundred years old,
claw, menace.
Frantic hair nests
waft in the breeze.
Sure I hear a cackle.

On pub verandas,
men in singlets,
slurp beer, swat flies,
boast how many roos they've shot.
At night, the stillness is fractured
by whoops, whistles,
cars revving.

A thin African woman
in a colourful scarf,
wheels her suitcase
covered in stickers,
joins our day tour
for a lift to Whitecliffs.
In a soft voice tells us
she bought land for ten thousand
and lived in a caravan
up until it melted.

An hour into the journey,
I put down my book
gaze out the window.
Crows gouge a roadside carcass.

Eruption

I am his target
         again.

He savaged the dividing fence
yelled threats, obscenities
and palings fell like wooden
ducks at the local fair.

The first time,
he savaged my security door
mangled my small tree
poured a sticky substance
over my newly painted brick fence
and rubbish
his rubbish
strewn across my pebbles.

I am the woman he loathes.
Everyday he sits
on his front veranda
arms folded
         watching.

Late at night
I hear noises
like furniture dragged
muffled sobs
once, a loud shriek.

His young son perches
on the edge of an upended trampoline
snivels in the chaos
of his front garden.
His wife never speaks,
head bowed
hemline sags.
She scurries,
she always scurries.

A neighbour says,
'He wouldn't do it
if you had a man.'

The Entertainer

He sways on a bench,
does his own cha cha,
ignores boots and beanie tourists
and bored locals
who've seen it all before.

He commands, carouses,
dips his yellow cap
gives a loud screech,
before he attacks
a piece of dry bread.

Wales – 1977

A Welsh whimsy

In Swansea,
our bed and breakfast host
gel-spiked hair
a cigarette droops
at the side of her mouth,
no hot water,
board across the bath,
a plumber who never comes
and a parrot that says,
'Toast *or* eggs.
Toast *or* eggs.'

I gaze at ramblers in raincoats
and sheep.
In the window,
a wasp tries to escape.

The Lift

Wind whooshes,
trees jive.
He lifts the bonnet
and peers inside.
'Are you mechanically minded?' I ask.
He grins, shakes his head, 'Not a bit.'
Voices dwindle,
the car park empties,
a dog howls,
a rustle in the bushes.
He rings the road service,
'They could be hours.'
I utter farewell
dart between trees
shrink from flying branches,
nearly trip on a stump
strands of hair whip my face.

A tall figure in a hood and boots approaches.
Leaves circle my feet,
paper scraps blow into the gutter.
Hood and boots draws closer.
I have no nail file,
no scissors.
lights, cars, safety,
I hail a taxi
and jump inside.
The driver turns.
I stifle a scream.

Was She?

Little girl, little girl.
She bent over me,
beads clacking,
perfume nauseous,
bulging eyes,
tall and bony.
Miss Bachelli
the art teacher,
had her favourites.

Was she eccentric? Was she crazy?
Or on permanent rehearsal
for a non-existent play.
I loved art,
finished a few sketches
and a still life painting,
passed an essay on Sidney Nolan,
to the clack of beads
and echoes of
Little girl, little girl.

The Decision

She's in mauve again.
blouse, headband, lipstick.
Tells me she knows
what happened to Schubert,
quaffs her double brandy,
sniffs and wipes a tear.
'He'd been missing for weeks.
Pest man found him
dead beneath the house. He was
ten, had thyroid trouble and he
never got along with the possum.'
She rolls her eyes, slurps her brandy.
'I haven't had the courage to move him,'
she pauses, 'and I'm still deciding
if I'll bury, cremate,
or just get him stuffed.'

Christmas Day 1971

'Jingle Bells' plays on the radio
to the splinter of walnuts.
Dad hoses the fiery tin roof,
Mum wipes her flushed face
with her green apron
prods the roast potatoes
checks the beef.
I sip a cold lemonade
scuff my sandals on the linoleum floor,
listen to the strange tongue of an
aunt, uncle and cousin,
I'd only met six months before.
Cards with snow and reindeer
decorate our kitchen cabinet.

I prance around the Christmas tree
Mum shouts, 'Don't you open the presents.'
My cousin grins, calls me, 'Kangaroo.'
His father boasts about the beautiful
wines and cheeses in France.
Mum snaps, 'So why didn't you stay there.'
My aunt and uncle whisper, straighten their party hats,
pull a cracker.

Trials

We spend our lives waiting
for buses, trains,
test results,
plants to grow,
planes to arrive
storms to end,
grief to lessen,
pain to disappear,
lovers to call.
And the verdict.

Glazed

I wade through lights, colour, noise
and the maze of machines.
Coats still on,
pasty skin,
body odour.

A woman hunches over her machine
sips on a cocktail, keeps tapping.
My partner plays two machines,
suggests I buy a drink,
tells me he won't be long.

A sudden yell.
Joy? Dismay?
Staff keep members plied with mini-quiches, pies.
I overhear, 'I'm dying to pee, but might get lucky.'
Her mate says, 'Should check my kid,
left him asleep in the car hours ago.'
'C'mon, Dad, let's go home,'
a middle-aged woman tugs
on her father's sleeve.
He snaps, 'I'm not ready.'

Bored, I drift into the all-night café.
Halfway through my drink
my partner appears,
hands in pockets, head bent.
I don't ask about his losses.

Targeted

Early evening neighbours cook
feed children, husbands, lovers,
five shots are fired.
He crumples, blood gushes,
gasps and gurgles.
Patrons rush from nearby café,
one tries to revive him,
another calls an ambulance.
He is dead.

Blue lights spin,
car doors slam
uniformed officer
sprints up the street.

Night detectives
pace, probe, pound on locked doors.
Day later, white coats forage,
journalists hover,
climb in and out vans
shoulder cumbersome cameras
smoke, chatter.

End of the week,
bouquet of flowers
and balloon of a Tigers head
tied to the telegraph pole
on my street corner.

A Dog's Life

Wall of hair
shields his face.
On his patch,
he sits cross-legged
head bent, furiously writing.
But what is he writing?
A poem, memoir, story
the reason why he is homeless?
His belongings are scattered,
dirt streaked jumper, large beanie,
can of soft drink and a few plastic bags.
He lifts his head,
gives his two fox terriers a hug.
One yawns, the other barks.

I dart into a store,
return with dog food, can opener and bowls.
But he and his terriers have gone.
Woman nearby doing street art grins at me.
I shrug, then place the items
beneath his large beanie.

Colour of Envy

Your perfect house
          husband
          body
          life.

Your trench coat
bought in Windsor, England
discarded after a single wear.
Your holiday in Venice.
The lover in Greece.

Your blouses I ironed,
your green stilettos
in a cupboard of their own.
Your Jaguar
your silk scarves,
crystal glasses,
jewellery.

And my calloused hands,
around your crumpled neck.

Captured

I prepare with precision
my corn-fed chicken breast
add onions, herbs, tomatoes
cup of stock
drizzle of oil.

Once cooked, I remove the skin,
slice the breast, take a bite,
the meat is dark, gamey,
I eat the onions and tomatoes instead.
What a disappointment. The last corn-fed
chicken was delicious.

I pause, reflect in the seventies
Dad told me about a workmate
called Timber. He had a mouth as
wide and as loud as the harbour.
Timber used to trap pigeons in the
rail freight yard, hand them over
to a go-between to sell as chickens for
restaurants in the city.

I was appalled. Didn't believe it.
Now, I'm not so sure.
Tomorrow, I'll make a cheese and spinach pie.

The Usual

Bare chest, work boots
sock under left armpit
walks his toy poodle.

One-eyed man in bowler hat
rides his skateboard
blows bubbles.

Woman sings 'Ave Maria'
pushes her barking dog
in a battered stroller.

Youth with green hair
frangipani behind his ear
juggles donuts.

I stare at the taxidermist's invoice
pour a green tea
hug my stuffed cat.

An Ending

soak up the sunset
stroke exquisite beads
mumble a mantra
listen to a dingo howl
observe a lone bather
and a child as he paddles

my final days
on wet sand

Impression

He tells me I have grey teeth.
I am indignant. 'Not all surely.
I've only had two root canals.'
Scanty hair, his stature frail,
'The colour will be hard to match.'
He blends a berry-coloured liquid,
looks like yogurt, in a small ceramic
bowl. He does his checks and measures.
The impression is ready. He inserts
the top first, waits a minute, then inserts
the bottom.

All this work for one tooth, I think.
He tells me to rinse with a fizzy pink
liquid, it tastes like cordial.
'The old tooth you made lasted years.'
I lick my lips, wipe sides of my mouth
with a tissue.
'The plate is jagged, that's why you have
lumps on your tongue.'
I ask him the price.
'Four hundred.' He blinks, hands me
my old tooth. 'Your new one will be
ready in a week.'
I notice his tremor.

A smudge of impression
on the lapel of his white coat.

Unanswered

I peer at inky sky,

with dexterity wrap each star,

flirt with infinity.

Yoga pose at dawn.

Discarded

A cleaner yawns,
mops spilt drink,
calls to her colleague
about their rostered night off.
Mouldy walls;
each room, a wardrobe,
single bed, a chair.

Frail figures
shift rugs over bony knees.
Some dribble. Some whisper.
A new resident chatters
about grandchildren
she never sees.

Close by, woman in red beret
boasts about the time she posed nude
for Picasso. Peers out the window.
Writes on the pane.
Where is my home?

Question of Faith

Dark-haired woman and I
wait in the bus shelter
we chat about the tardy service
and the moody weather.

I query her accent,
'I'm from El Salvador
arrived here in '49.
Had to raise four children,
on my own.
One of my girls is a barrister,
my boy is a doctor,
and the others are doing well too.'
She straightens the comb in her bun.

'Do you have family in El Salvador?' I ask.
'Yes, but it's not safe to go back. The secret
police took my brother in the night. I never
saw him again. Drug barons patrol the
streets. And the poverty…' she sighs.
Raises her hands and continues, 'Twice a
a week I clean for Maria, a Greek lady.
She sings sad songs and strums a guitar.
Sometimes we sit in her courtyard and I have
a short black. She told me how she suffered
under the junta. Her husband was so badly
tortured, he died.'

She leans closer. I smell her light perfume.
'Maria drinks too much whiskey. Smokes too
too many cigarettes. I offer to read her the Bible,
but she never wants to listen.' She hands me a
card. 'Please come to Bible study.'

I don't reveal my own years of fear
under Salazar's regime.
Whispered threats.
Knocks on the door.
In Lisbon, my neighbour,
a professor of semantics, was dragged
from his home, screaming.
The church knew.

Bus approaches.
When she's not looking, I scrunch
her card. Toss it into the nearby bin.

Norfolk Island Elegy

No street lights.
No traffic lights.
Cows stroll freely,
as hens bustle
across roads, along footpaths.
At night, tropical rains
bruise my motel windows.
In next door's café,
young Kiwi calls me 'Honeybunch,'
and serves me eggs on toast
to the tune of 'Daddy Cool'.

Bus tours whisk visitors
around the island.
Political questions
are quickly silenced,
except for one driver,
'We are now ruled by the mainland,
it's divided us locals. We have to
pay council rates, but never get our
bins emptied.'
That's as much as he will say.

Waves pummel rocks
I wander the cemetery.
See prisoners in bloodstained rags
fingernails claw at filthy cell walls,
a guard sniggers.

Ghosts linger.
Pine trees sigh.

The Piranha and the Porpoise

Welcome to Rio
city of *favelas*
buckets for waste,
candles for light
one tap at the end of the street,
cabbage and potato soup
diet for the poor.

At traffic lights, boys with scabby knees,
dart between cars, lean inside windows,
mimic, beg. Pickpockets leer in doorways,
as bandits surround suited man,
snatch his attaché case, punch his face.
Jobless youth hurls a rock through a shop
window. He yells about the money spent
on the Olympics.

Bikini-clad tourists
sip cocktails
on hotel verandas
dance to the samba.

Thousands march,
'Save our homes.
Boycott the Games.'

Gunshot.
Scream.
Welcome to Rio.

Guatemala

Boy of nine helps his mother to make
stew, she haggles, begs, steals,
for her five younger children.
Men with guns, harsh voices,
abducted their father in the night.
Her friends, husbands, sons,
met the same fate.

An honest judge was killed.
Civilians too afraid,
whisper secrets, huddle in laneways.
Graveyards crammed with the
resentful, innocent,
generals rant about democracy
order death squads
to shoot street children.

Head Start

Killed by the suave dentist
with his sunglasses,
cravat and American drawl.
Head to be a trophy
on another hunter's wall.
The assassin's excuse,
'I didn't know he was
the famous Cecil.'

I join the protestors,
'Fine him heavy,
close his practice.'
Vent my rage on Twitter, Facebook.

But is this punishment enough?

I take lessons in archery,
ply the dentist with drinks,
lure him to the scrub.
Give him a head start.
Aim the arrow into his back,
watch him fall, writhe, scream.
'Remember Cecil.'

In the distance,
the roar of a lion.

Memento

Spicy

Curry
incense
serpentine alleys
and your sequinned sari
wafting in the breeze.

Shrewish

Cheap perfume
leather skirt
and the raucous voice
from the bottle blonde
next door.

Sensual

Silk slippers
aromatherapy oils
and the night you and I
tangoed topless
beside the pool.

Green

My weatherboard house,
the upholstered sofa, cupboards,
nineteen seventies telephone
and the lamp on top of the TV.

Green blouse, coat, bag,
Mother's beads,
Father's watchband.
Dried paint on brushes,
My Persian's collar.

As a child,
on St Patrick's Day,
Mother made sure I wore
a green ribbon.

The scarf you threw around your neck,
the last time I saw you.

Festering

Her words acrid,
on one unlined page
green envelope. Deliberate?

My questions answered.
Her interpretation, blaming me
for another's behaviour
years ago.

Where has her affection gone?
I slip the page into the envelope.
Stare at the stamp, Royal Mail Supports
Cancer UK.

She can wait for my reply.

Fractured

Fusty, arms dangle,
fingernails chewed, dirty.

Swish of robes
smell of incense
as a livid priest
carrying his chalice
flees upstairs.

We face each other,
roll eyes.
Nance tosses bedclothes aside,
totters on bandaged legs,
'Bugger him, bugger him.'
She gives me a sly wink
on the back of her nightie
is a damp patch.
'Didn't the Gestapo change you today?'

Glass breaks,
somebody cries, 'No fruit again.'
Nance scratches her unwashed hair.

I beat a pillow.

Midnight Mender

She peers out
at rushing cabs
dog walker with mauve hair
skinny girl blowing up a balloon.

Down the hall,
voices, laughter,
and the smell of minestrone soup.
She crouches on her stool
smooths down the trousers,
                    his trousers,
squints as she threads the needle.
Her first time in New York,
she squirms at her cousins' efforts
to show her the sights,
They don't realise I'm here to mend,
to mend my husband's trousers.

She never told anyone he went missing.
Her suitcase filled with ten pairs of trousers,
                    his trousers,
packet of rusted needles
reels of knotted cotton.

She rises at noon
does her daily crossword
buys her few groceries,
over the road.

At midnight she returns to her mending,
curses
as she notices a red stain
on the inside of the left pocket,
                    his left pocket.
Yesterday's mistake.

Airless

Sea sprinkles
her patent leather shoes
as gulls perform
their sky aerobics.

Her mother
always in bed
feeble voice
limbs wasted.

Nurses in starched caps
starched faces
carry bowls
her father
drinks too much
plays his music.

Her older sister moved away
brief phone call
hastily scrawled note.

In the distance
she hears a flute.

Stormy Weather

She feeds the lorikeets,
then, armed with a bucket, cloth,
positions the ladder with care
close to the window.

Waves to a neighbour,
hums to 'Stormy Weather'.

Later, she sips
a cup of warm water,
inhales on a cigarette.
Throws her blue cardigan
over a chair.

On the radio
bomb blast in Karachi.

She squeezes out the cloth,
and broods on that sealed letter
from her ex-husband.

A Pause in the Sun

He grows lettuce, tomatoes, zucchini,
has a scarecrow, fig trees
and several pumpkins on his roof.

His granddaughter,
in shorts, T-shirt, sunscreen,
chatters as she plays in the dirt.

He closes his eyes,
remembers another garden,
a village, houses with cement floors.

In outdoor cafés,
men gather,
drink thick black coffee,
study their cards,
as hefty women balance
baskets of washing on their heads.

Chickens scatter,
laughter erupts,
as a goat escapes from a broken fence.

He opens his eyes,
smiles at his granddaughter,
who stands before him.
Small hands cupped,
she slowly sprinkles dirt,
into his lap.

An Orthodox Easter Mass

Outside the church
in balmy air,
midnight worshippers
whisper, hold candles,
chastise children
as the priest utters mass.

In black,
worshippers scrutinise each others'
clothes, jewellery,
as candle flames flicker
in the gentle breeze.
A child is hoisted
upon her father's shoulders,
her candle almost singes his hair.

Frail bespectacled man,
fumbles with his tie
old woman yawns,
as two young women
compare last night's dates.

Shortly, into the mass,
worshippers peer at watches,
kiss each others lips, cheeks,
bless themselves before they leave.

Disappearing Gondolas

Gondola glides
along Venice canals,
past crumbling medieval mansions,
dark-haired women,
peg clothes, laugh, chatter,
shake mats over balconies.

My fingers caress the water,
while the velvety-voiced gondolier
speaks of Venice, its history.

A masked child waves,
the gondolier smiles
then says,
he has three children,
a wife and sick mother.

A motor launch
with boisterous tourists
speeds by.

He is still smiling
as I close my eyes.

Adrenalin

'You know Gadaffi has been in power for forty-two years.
Forty-two years. I was eight when he became our leader.'
He turns away from the microphone, spits in the dirt.
My niece got interrogated by the secret police
and my father shot by a sniper. This place is crazy.'
He shakes his head.

I nod, he continues, 'But here if you gather, you are
seen as subversive. An opponent of the regime.
Then one day your family, friends, go missing. In parts
of Tripoli we have no electricity, running water.
My cousin was in solitary confinement.
Now he has no toenails.'

I glance across the road at a woman in a hijab.
Utility roars past, the men in bloodied bandannas
narrow their eyes. Small pebbles skim my ankles.

I smell smoke, cough,
'It's not safe to talk any more.'
He turns on his heel.

My cameraman curses,
we hear approaching gunfire.
I bite my lip
run for cover.

Blanket Trampling Summers

in the bath
we trampled blankets
mum talked about an episode
in the *I Love Lucy Show*
where the actors had to trample
grapes for a job
we stamped in the middle
then up one end down the other
I wriggled my toes
nudged blanket corners
the water was cool
in that january heat
when mum was satisfied
we pulled the plug rinsed and
rinsed again
took turns to sit on the bath's edge
had a short break
we squeezed then heaved the blankets
into a tin tub lifted it at either end and headed
into the yard lowered the hills hoist as
far down as it went and threw the sodden
blankets over   I handed mum the pegs and
wiped the sweat from my brow

in later years there was no more
washing blankets in the bath
mum used to throw them over the clothes line
and beat them free of dust with a stick

now I take the blankets
to the dry cleaners

Market by Moonlight

She tosses her plait
offers me trinkets,
straightens her sari
of midnight blue.
He sits cross-legged
strokes bottles of dubious liquid
teeth tainted a reddish brown
men in tunics, barter.
Giddy with aromas of garlic, spices,
I wander to the stall opposite
skinny dog sniffs the ground.
I jump nearby an explosion,
teenage boy polishing boots says,
'It's only our neighbours, we're close to Kashmir.'
Child with jam-smeared face
rushes up to me,
curls sticky fingers
around my pampered hand.

Ragtime

Ragged mounds cough, twitch,
nearby, upturned sneakers, no laces.
Ragged woman in a beanie
leans against tunnel wall
pulls out her false teeth
blows a toy whistle.
Ragged boy in skull-and-crossbones T-shirt,
plays 'The Entertainer' on his violin,
younger boy wolfs fists of lollies.
The woman yells, 'Ya pinched them didn't ya!'
She giggles, wags a wounded finger.
Two mounds awake, throw off doonas
stretch, nod to one another,
scramble inside backpacks
for white knights, black knights,
and a ragged chessboard.

Kitchen Echoes

My new wooden spoon doesn't fit
in my seventies drawer,
            harbours
'Have you washed your hands?
'Don't forget Grace before dinner.'

Cupboards too high, too low, too small.
My frypan wedges on the bottom shelf,
beside two green bowls;
Mum had made whipped cream in
and scones that used to disappoint.

Modern spatula hangs on a nail,
to the right of a single sink.
I peer in the drawer,
battered whisk
rusted tea strainer.

Fingering utensils, I hear Dad's voice,
'Haven't you done your homework yet?'

Foundations

They're demolishing
the house next door,
roof, walls, floor.
I still hear
a piano tinkle
swing creak
children giggle.

I shared secrets with the girls,
fought with their brothers
envied their scooters
made lucky dips wrapped in newspaper
for a small fee,
spent my earnings on sherbets and chips.

Soon, two townhouses
will be built on the site
where I painted my nails
discarded my doll
smoked my first cigarette.

Picnic

She scuffs at sand

Remembers

At seven
she drifts
from the picnic
when the man
emerges from the scrub
speaks, makes a grab
for her hand.

Savage dreams.
She sleeps
in her parents' bed
for weeks.
His beard
gap in the teeth.

Remembers

In the sixties
a three-year-old girl
went missing here.

She broods
on that absent child
shivers
sleeps with the light on.

Best Friends

The factory's still there
with that steep concrete drive
where you and I used to play
as we waited for your mother
to finish work. Sometimes, if the boss
was out we'd sneak into the factory,
cover our ears and gaze at the women
bent over knitting machines
sweat matted hair and eyebrows
that met in the middle.
I'd stroke the coloured wool
you accused me once of stealing
one long strand
and I was sent to Coventry.

I denied the theft
we didn't speak for weeks.
You spoke first, said you were sorry,
then told me you and your family
were returning to Italy.
The evening before your departure,
my father set up the tape recorder,
and your grandmother, a lover of food and wrestling,
sang to us.

She laughed about the time she caught me
adding soap powder to her cooking.

You promised to write.
I knew you wouldn't.

In Passing

she looks at me
smiles
an announcement
        train delayed twenty minutes
we sigh
i used to live around here she says
now i'm in the country on a small farm
I nod
we came from Yugoslavia i was sixteen
going to study medicine but got married at nineteen
to please my father
was it arranged I think but don't pry
we worked hard bought a house my husband had
schizophrenia he died two years ago
now young ones want luxuries we had secondhand
furniture and no car for years
one of my son's is on drugs he's always looking for money
he was in jail once and didn't even go to his father's funeral
the other son gambles day and night at the casino
she throws up her hands I nod again
my daughter's nearly thirty-five dyes her hair purple
look's like I'll never be a grandmother
i can't understand my kids

are you married she asks then offers me a pear
the train arrives
it's been good talking to you

Beyond the Yellow Line

two girls
one no more than eleven twelve
hair mussy
is wrapped in a blanket

the younger girl
            are they sisters
wheels a small case
they saunter down the platform
i glance around for parents
assistant tells me
            we see those kinds of kids passing through
            here all the time   said they're heading west
            west where   i think   are they fleeing abuse

i watch as the older girl shrugs off the blanket
before she steps onto the train
guard blows the whistle

the younger one strikes a match
sets the blanket alight

The Great Divide

Every morning
he hunches in the corner
grimy fingers   grimy life
curls around a cardboard cup.
His head is bent
perhaps in prayer
other times he stares
at passing suits   stilettos
hears words he doesn't follow.

Today he gives a strangled cry
throws his cardboard cup
at a parked car
sniggers as dregs slide down the door.
Wraps his blanket
tightly round him
sways from side to side.

One passing stiletto whispers to another
'Loser.'

By Friday lunchtime
he's gone.

Blithe

My old boots, medium brown,
pointed toes, low heels,
are often admired.

When quizzed about their age,
I grin at shocked faces, rolled eyes.
My boots match my coat,
patched corduroys,
and socks with gaping holes.

My boots have marched in rallies,
scaled craggy hills,
sprinted on wet sand.
They played privy to my flirting
with a handsome policeman, as he
wrote me out a ticket.
My boots have been on retreat,
days of tofu, silence.
And they observed my angst,
withdrawals from chocolate.

My boots have celebrated
a great nephew's bar mitzvah
a sister's engagement.

And every week
my boots crunch pebbles underfoot,
as I carry a posy of flowers
to my parents' grave.

Money First

In Paraguay
poor women grumble above muzak
about price rises
snap at fidgety children
as husbands, lovers,
with bored expressions
push trolleys
carry bags.

Someone shouts 'Fire!'
people cough
children bawl
smoke fills
the shopping centre
crowds race to exits
doors locked
people, eyes streaming,
beg, claw,
at security staff
to let them out.

Hundreds are dead
others in hospital.
The mall owner denies
he ordered the doors locked
so customers had to pay before leaving.

A charred baby's shawl
lies among the ashes.

Tasting Salt

I recline
in my living room
watch reports:

Aged Afghan men
rummage through debris
women in burquas, squat, sway.

Young Iraqi men
raise fists, voices,
set fire to an American flag.

White House president
preaches on human rights
offers asylum to Pinochet:
bodies in unmarked graves
children begging in a Santiago street.

National Front
march through London,
shaven heads, swastikas on T-shirts
carrying placards, 'Refugees out.'

In Sudan, militia, some only boys
sneer, cradle guns, bazookas
dog roams village
silent, empty.

I close my eyes
taste salt.

Compulsion

His retirement spent
cleaning
hoovering
mopping
sweeping
wiping chandeliers
tops of wardrobes, walls.

His sister the same.

When they were children
their father would beat them
if his boots weren't polished
dresser not dusted
stairs not swept.

'Why didn't our mother leave him?'
He nearly killed her once.'

They never sought help
everyone else filthy,
everyone else living in dirt.

Clean, clean,
erase the bruises.

Clean, clean,
erase the pain.

Latte Lives

At the small café
we settle in our chairs
rub hands.
Viola examines the menu,
gives a sigh.
'My daughter has a new boyfriend.
A mechanic. He's all right I suppose
but don't think he's *the one.*
She's almost forty and wants a baby.
He doesn't want kids and they argue a bit too.'

A woman in a tattered beanie approaches us.
She holds out her hand, asks for money. I refuse politely.
She screeches, waves her arms, stomps away.
'She needs to be cared for. Shouldn't go about annoying people.
Where's her family? Think I'll just have a skim latte.' Viola says,

'Maybe she doesn't have anyone.' I decide on hot chocolate, raisin toast.
'Paid another five hundred to my lawyer yesterday. This battle
with my ex is turning into a circus. He lost all his money
on the share market.' Viola rubs her eyes.

More screeching. Beanie woman hurries past. Shoppers stare.
'It's sad. Bet she's homeless.' I pat my lips with a serviette.
Viola drains her coffee, glances at her watch.
'I've got a casserole cooking
in my new crockpot.'
I nod, butter my second piece of toast.
A few moments of silence.
Viola stands. 'I'd better go. See you at yoga.'

She disappears among the Thursday night crowd.
Beanie woman now abuses the florist.

A Memory Blush

Today I buy a rouge.
My last, peach colour, dulcet scent,
was bought in Lisbon decades ago,
by Sebastian, my father's cousin.
Slim, with a Beatles haircut,
he came from Venezuela.

I was unwell. 'Women's troubles' my father
whispered to his cousin, as they left me
to rest in the hotel.

On their return, Sebastian hands me the rouge,
indicates my wan face. My father tells me about
their afternoon – lunch of potatoes and sardines,
as they listened to *The Fado* and laughed as a
watch peddler was chased by police.

Less than twelve months
after our Lisbon stay
we heard Sebastian had a fatal heart attack.
He was in his early forties.

I kept his gift for years,
think about him often as I lightly
brush the rouge onto my cheeks.

risk taker

early morning
pink streaked hair
squats in the mall's entrance
sips a can of beer
shoppers glance   snigger
then bustle on

by lunchtime
she sprawls on a bench
khol eyes
lip stud bleeds
she takes off one shoe
aims it at a gloating bystander
knocks off his wig

Moods of Malice

He guzzles from a bottle
in a brown paper bag
then takes a drag on his cigarette.
She sprawls on doorstep
blonde hair greasy, black roots visible
as barefoot toddler sucks on dummy,
plays with dead cockroach.

He looks across at two storey villa
bars on windows, Doberman behind gate
and the woman in high heels
who sits on her balcony
smoking.

No Reason

Cat without ears
outside a crumbling house
flinches as I pass.

One legged seagull
surrounded by broken bottles
ignores me
as I pass.

Scruffy man
in rolled up trousers
and no shoes
winks as I pass.

Anomaly.

Witness

He stands
frayed collar, cuffs,
has a word, shares a joke,
with the checkout girl.
Pays for
a loaf of bread,
a wedge of cheese
a carton of milk.

Outside, a threadbare dog drools
he pours milk into a saucer.
Shoppers slam car doors
bicker with partners,
a child in a dirty dress
sucks her thumb, lags behind.

He settles on the bench
waves to a security guard,
forages through his cigarette butts,

opens a mouldy copy of

War and Peace.

Rosa

'Do my son and daughter
know I'm here?'
She hugs me, rubbing tear-filled eyes,
her hair needs washing,
her cardigan is stained.

Where is that smartly dressed woman, the tailor's wife,
with the earrings, the hat?
Was it only a few years ago
when we caught the same bus?
Her English was poor, but we managed,
even had a laugh or two.
She twists her handkerchief,
and in between sobs, tells me
she's only fed sandwiches
has no money.
She lifts the leg of her slacks,
her ankle is swollen.

I can't speak.

Down the hall, a male voice shouts,
'I'm getting out tomorrow.'
A woman opposite us
wipes the already clean table,
'I shouldn't be in here.'

A nurse with a fixed smile
walks past.

A male voice shouts,
'I'm getting out tomorrow.'

Passage

Dribble,
wither.

Middle-aged son
feeds his silent mother
flustered wipes food from her chin.

Opposite
eyepatch woman
thumps table
mutters
rocks to and fro.

Nearby
shrunken, mottled hands clasped
shirt buttons unfastened
slumps in his chair.

Staff
walk briskly
smile at visitors
clear debris, wipe tables
deliver trays.

In the hall
painters, laugh and chatter,
vacuum cleaner switches on.

Dribble,
wither.

Tango to Forget

As genteel couples
tango in an open air plaza of Buenos Aires
enraged mobs, pound on locked bank doors
demanding their money
so they can escape
to America, Canada, anywhere,
seeking security, education for their children
a steadfast existence
as transitory presidents
conceal truth
hide in luxury.

In the slums of Buenos Aires,
the destitute
scavenge in trash heaps
a mouldy sandwich
half-bottle of drink.

As evening approaches,
bystanders gather
watch genteel couples
tango.

As mine once did

I now sleep
in what was my parents' room.
On certain nights
sleep eludes me.
Is it the heat?
my disquiet?
Blinds partly open
street light sneaks in
I face my dressing table mirror
stare as tree branches
dance a pattern on my wardrobe.

I hear crying
from next door's little girl.
Will her parents rush
to give her a cuddle
tell her stories about princes, paupers,
as mine once did?
Voices ask if I can draw the Apple Fairy
warn Snow White about the wicked queen.
In the forest I dart between the trees,
follow the breadcrumb trail with Hansel and Gretel.

Mum's lips brush my forehead
her lavender perfume infuses the room.
Dad's calloused hands
caress my wet cheeks.
I close my eyes,
and remember to search
for the missing glass slipper.

The Maybe Country

Young widows watch
scraggy children
play among rubble.
Donkey coat bloodied
pulls a loaded cart.

Dusty turban,
dusty tunic,
picks at yellowed toenails,
utters profanities,
as bearded figures
hover in alleyways.
Smoke. Whisper. Spit.

Teenage boy throws stones
yells at foreign troops.
His sister hobbles beside him,
her leg lost to a landmine.

Kabul, once the city of music, laughter,
women with education, careers,
choices to remain single,
choices to marry.

Then the Russians,
later the Taliban,
next the Coalition of the Willing.

Forget indignation.
Forget platitudes.
This is habitual.
What hope Afghanistan.

Haunted

Old man raises his hat
to friends, strangers,
jiggles his great-grandchildren upon his knee.

Deny
Deny

Some nights,
he tosses, turns,
hears the screams of his victims
wipes the sweat from his face,
covers his ears.

Deny
Deny

He stares at the television,
as German soldiers
drive Jews from their homes.
They beat one youth
with the butt of a rifle,
kick another in the head.

He combs his sparse white hair,
straightens his cravat.
Blows a kiss to his daughter.

Deny
Deny

Sure Thing

he parks his shabby pram
next to the pole
outside the betting shop

inside he perches on a stool
grunts at the television
the race caller roars
the punters scrutinise form guides
masticate pens
they were in here yesterday
and the day before

beard growth
nudges him
I've gotta tip mate
it's a sure thing

he nods
rushes to place the bet
moments later
he curses
crumples his betting slip
looks out the window

his pram is gone

Check Mate

Long queue
at the post office
mousey hair
trench coat
turns to me mutters,
'Awful weather for summer isn't it?'
'Yes,' I reply, 'but I prefer it to the heat.'
She removes her glasses, gives them a quick wipe.

'I've just been to see my husband, he's in a
nursing home, had a stroke. I really miss him.
He was also very handy, did all the repairs around the
house. And he loved his chess.'
We move forward a few steps.
'My husband is older than me, but such a handsome man,
he doesn't look his age. I go to see him every day.'

'Does he still know you?'

She shakes her head, eyes brim with tears. Forages inside her
bag pulls out her purse. 'Days aren't too bad it's the nights
I hate.'

We move again.

'But lately,' she leans closer, lowers her voice, 'I've been
getting some strange phone calls. Whoever it is hangs up, but
once a woman spoke, she had an accent and asked for my
husband. Told her he's in a nursing home. She abused me,
called me horrible names. And I'm sure I heard a child crying
in the background.'

'Next please.'

Centre Stage

Pirates in blue kerchiefs
banter to each other
as they hurtle me
along corridors
around corners
into lifts.

Gowns swish
masked figures hover.
The protagonist, manner jovial
reminds me of my uncle.
I am led into the theatre.
Commands, lights, props,
my players are waiting
my stomach churns.

The protagonist smiles,
'You will relax soon.'
His assistant inserts a needle
in the back of my hand.

1956

She tells me about the six o'clock swill,
the elbows, the shoves, the fights,
beer-stained white vests,
stench of stale sweat,
and a slang she doesn't understand:
Sheila, struth, crikey.
Her workmate, a cheeky barmaid
who idolised James Dean.

Dust-clogged nostrils, eyelids, throat,
savage flies, savage heat,
mosquitoes that tore
at her flesh, her mind.

Rented room,
dressing table, speckled mirror
a wardrobe door
that wouldn't stay shut.

Her escape from Adelaide,
a husband with a drinking problem
church cliques with tightly permed hair.

A yearning for her mother,
and a windy seaport in England's north-west.

Then she tells me with a wistful sigh,
about a curly-haired cane cutter,
who asked for a shandy in broken English.
My father.

Platform Performance

She stands
flicking cigarette ash
onto the tracks.
'Please move away from edge of platform.'
She looks around
overcast day
people on seats, reading, knitting,
some staring into space.
She takes off sunglasses,
fingers tug at leopard-skin tights,
toe nails painted red.

Train approaches,
'Please move away from edge of platform.'
She tosses her sunglasses onto the tracks.

Bystanders gasp,
she skips away.

Elephants' Grief

They gather
trunks scuff at dust
baby cringes, sidles closer
to mother's warm flank.

In the distance, an engine,
squeal of brakes,
'No not again!'
a gouged carcass rots.

No tusks.
No tusks.

At markets,
slaughter money
changes hands.

Truck is stopped
at the Malaysian border
driver pleads for clemency.

In Shanghai,
a tea merchant
caresses his ivory.

On the Cusp

The cleaners have gone
with their squeaky trolley
and gossip about
the man upstairs.

She eyes her suitcase
ponders on her
gear in storage,
runs a finger along
the flat-screen television
her mobile signals a text:

buy a unit
before money
runs out
              deb

Every few days
her sheets and towels are washed
no electricity, gas, or water bills,
and a microwave to heat her meals.

>   *I don't miss my house*
>   *except for the cool breeze*
>   *I used to get*
>   *whenever I'd open the front door.*

Her days drift,
few hours on the pokies
bets on the keno,
what's the harm?
she knows when to stop.

She tells anyone who listens
how busy she is
calls her motel room 'my unit'
at four hundred and forty a week.

Long Interlude

A strange man
asked for you the other day
reckons he knew you
acted weird.

I was puzzled. What did he look like?

Slim, grey hair, scruffy,
carried a bike helmet
and was a bit stooped.

Stooped? He used to be solid
lifted car trailers with one hand
always boasted about his strength
knowledge of acupuncture
love of his fellow man.

Stooped I pondered.

My thoughts are interrupted.

He wanted to know
if you are seeing anyone
have a boyfriend?
says you took
a restraining order against him.

Eleven years
since the break-up.

Survive or Die

Illegals drown
picking cockles
in a Lancashire bay.

Steel sea
snatches
doesn't discriminate
doesn't choose.

They were promised
housing, work, education,
no more living in caves, tents,
uncertainty, incursion, fear.

Another boatload
of illegals
due tomorrow
smugglers
arrange lives
arrange payment.

Don't Tell

skittle legs mutters
leans against her gate
stares at passing lollipop-licker
with bruise on right cheek

smeared mascara   scurries
yells into mobile phone
pushes empty pram

sunglasses   walking stick
exits house
whispers to skittle legs
takes her by the hand
gently guides her up path

moments   before they go inside
he gives a bellow
hits her with his stick

opposite   in the park
scrawny dog vomits

Man from Milan

Clean shaven,
fair-haired stranger
waits at bus stop
asks about timetables
says he's from Milan.
Morning is bitter
I huddle in my coat.
He tells me his city is colder.

He rents an apartment not far from mine
likes swimming, playing squash,
bushwalking and dancing.

Backpacked through Europe, same as me
discover we have similar tastes in wines too.
Should I give him my number?
I fumble for a pen.
He signals a cab, 'Hope my date waits for me.'
Then kisses the back of my hand.

A Bad Taste

Dusky like a hobbit cave, smell of wood smoke,
I watch as staff in long dresses, white bonnets,
scurry.

No alcohol, a variety of juices,
busy with tourists and folk
up for the day from Sydney.

I had the pear slice and soy ice cream.
'I'll come again when I'm next
in the mountains,' I tell a humble waitress.

Weeks later I see a newspaper article,
religious sect linked to owners of hobbit café.
Several on charges for abuse of forty children,
women not allowed to cut their hair,
denied contraception.

The pear slice tastes stale.
Ice cream curdles in my stomach.

Final Departure

Mourners enter
incense burning
silence.

Bow
settle into pews
elderly mourner
adjusts her scarf
others muffle sobs
into tissues.

Pastor strokes his robe
as pretty butterfly lands
on ledge of stained-glass window.

Outside
grey cars, dark suits arrive
funeral starts at noon.

Transient

His smile frail
skin sallow
delicate fingers
tap on arm of antique chair.

He swallows slowly,
desires dwindling
worships his collection of classics
red suede box
back of partner's head.

Dark ponytail
torn T-shirt
suntanned arms
paces lounge
stops at window
fidgets with blind.

He wonders
how long
this partner will stay.

The Memory Tree

I pass my old high school,
the grounds, now covered in grass,
large water tank and scribbly gums.

I recall one tree
splintered seats
that encircled its trunk,
acne, food trapped between braces.
We gossiped about teachers, pop idols,
as we ate our lunches
out of brown paper bags.

'Where's your beret?'
reprimands our headmistress,
powdered cheeks and brandy breath.

Plastic sports mats grated across gravel
by girls in archaic bloomers,
who smirked as other students
were chased from toilets for smoking.

I near the end of the school fence.
A boy swings on the gate,
'Hey lady, my class planted a tree today.'

Morning Mission

Toes like knotted rope
dress with a jagged hem.
On her head is a man's trilby
wispy hair blows in the breeze.
Wasn't she the seamstress
who had a pet rooster?

Cheeks on fire,
high blood pressure
or heavy rouge?
She tugs her shabby trolley
over cigarette butts, spit.

Outside the bank she stops,
takes a wad of notes from her trolley
then joins the queue.

Dual Madness

Repeatedly she
calls him a dog
throws food scraps
under his bed   then laughs
his hair matted
he hasn't shaved for weeks.

He flees home
wanders city streets
sleeps on park benches.

Last month he spoke
to anyone who'd listen
about his depression,
wanting to commit suicide.

Other homeless stare
police van cruises past
he hides behind a tree.

His mother over eighty
leaves the gas on
can't remember her name at times
or where she lives.
Sobs to neighbours
'Why did my son leave?'

Mobile Mania

Friends gasp in horror
'What! You don't have a mobile.
How do you cope? Survive?

'I don't need one. I'll only get a mobile
if my camel goes on strike, or I am chased
by Tibetan monks high on green tea.'

'But you need one, if you're late for an
appointment, job interview,
or even just meeting a friend.'

In buses, trains, shopping queues,
that invasive noise will erupt.
Once I yelled at a pink-haired teenager
'Can't you turn that stupid thing off!'

Mothers wheeling prams, couples walking dogs,
even the elderly have succumbed.
I fume, hiss, raise my eyes,
want to snatch their mobiles
and stamp on them.

But what a disaster if their mobile
is stolen, missing, or worse still left at home.

Now, digital cameras and iPods
are next on my hit list.

The Skinflint

She never had much
to do with him
he'd been next door for years.

Then she heard
how he'd suddenly died
on the way to hospital
a clot on the spine.

She remembered his stinginess
his wife wearing cast-offs
the times he was drunk, obnoxious,
on his homemade wine.

There were few mourners,
she went because his daughter
was an old school friend.

His widow,
still in cast-offs,
sits at the table, sings to herself
and sips the last of his homemade wine.

Just as guilty

Ten minutes before closing
shoppers dwindle
staff check registers.

We browse
she sighs
fingers the earrings,
places a string of red beads
around her young neck.

She grins, whispers,
'C'mon, let's leave.'
I tap her shoulder,
'What about the beads?
She keeps walking
I scan shoppers, staff,
mouth dry, heart thudding.
Outside, we flee to the station.

Years later
and continents apart
we still laugh
at not getting caught.

Rain and Reminisce

Corrimal

In a leaky caravan
I watch my parents play cards
picnic tables are empty
of food, gulls, crumbs.
At night, the rain stops
we stroll through dimly lit streets
Mum with a blanket round her shoulders
mud squelches between our toes.
The only corner shop is open
we join the rumpled queue
order chocolate hearts.

Batemans Bay

Dad nags Mum to wear lipstick.
I am urged to have my hair
cut very short, even though I pleaded.
Car gets bogged
Mum and Dad argue.
I kick legs, giggle
milk truck tows us out.

Katoomba

Snug inside our Austin
we drive towards the Blue Mountains
in rain and fog so thick
we could barely see ahead.
Dad's sister and her husband
gesticulate, talk
while Mum and I play I Spy.

Paris

Rain teems.
In a small café
Mum orders tea, but didn't know
the French for milk
until a young man, maybe a student
interprets to the puzzled waiter.

Warragamba Dam

I yawn, wipe sleep from eyes
scamper in and out between showers
pack picnic chairs, plastic cups,
and the portable gas stove into the car.
Mum refuses to go
I can still hear Dad's voice,
'It won't be raining when we get there.'

Defeat

They beach
themselves again
off Tasmania's coast
New Zealand's coast
hundreds surrender
life ebbs
some eyes open
some eyes close.

Scientists speech
The whales lost direction
no mention of
oil and chemical spills
and sonar waves
that ravage their senses.

Rescues fail,
liberators, some wipe tears
others yell, clutch sides of their heads.

Last fluke quivers
last eye closes.

Sameness

He grips wheel
scowls
sweat oozes.

She fidgets with bra strap
yawns, gazes out window
catches another male driver's eye
children in back seat
quarrel over new toys.

Sameness approaches
her in-laws
their subtle questions
warm beer
too neat house.

Disconnect

he slumps
in shadowed doorway
backpack at his feet
heedless of stampeding traffic

mangy dog
with bloody paw
noses a syringe on pavement

as business suits
carrying attaché cases
shout down mobile phones
intent on going to
he yawns
lays head on knees

shaved head   tattoos
spits
boots syringe into gutter

Tuesday's Class

He stalks the campus corridors
voices whisper 'Seek and ye shall find'
explodes into the classroom
startles teachers, students.

Spatter of bullets
bodies scramble for cover
chairs, desks overturned
glass shatters
blood trickles down window panes, walls.

Was the assassin also a victim?
A veteran from Vietnam, Iraq.
Had water forced down his throat
lit cigarettes stubbed across his back.

Yes Mr President
hand on heart,
let's go shopping
buy a gun
toy for a bored teenager.

Thirty-three killed in the classroom slaughter.
Fifty a day in Iraq.

Leaving

He strums a guitar
gives a sheepish grin
then places it against the wall.
I sip my tea.

He lights a cigarette,
turns, blows smoke out the window.
I gaze at packed boxes, shoes in plastic
bags, magazines neatly piled in the corner.
'I've only got a week before I move,' she says.

He fidgets, stubs out his cigarette.
'I haven't found a place yet. I've got to go
check out another flat.' He flicks through the
pages of a book, 'I like to read.'

She tells me she wants to make jewellery,
hire a market stall.
He jumps up, she hands him a jacket, helps his
thin arms into the sleeves.

For a moment, she and I don't speak,
listen to the distant yells of children
and the knocking from next door.

'He hasn't even tried to find work
and we always argue over money.'
I nod, walk across to the window.

In the alley, he stops to stroke a white cat.

Home

There she is
matted hair
mismatched clothes
pushing two shopping trolleys
laden with her chattels
round the park.

She snarls
waves her arms at ibis
oblivious to children's giggles
and adult stares.

Was she someone's
wife? Mother?

Did she once have
a home? Job?

Does she choose
to live in the park
collect rubbish
claim her space.
Ignore men playing chess
toddlers in the sandpit
lovers on benches.

At dusk
intruders vanish
to home, routine, safety.

Frayed coat
round her shoulders
she curls up beside
her laden trolleys.

The Diddy Men

They arrived
in a straw-laden box
when I was ten,
a present from my Irish Grandmother.
Mum carefully unwrapped
the brown paper, undid the sticky tape.
She lifted out two small plastic dolls,
one gripped his trouser belt
the other gripped his waistcoat,
both wore ties and had protruding teeth.
One foot was loose,
'Soon fix that,' said Dad.
I giggled at their large boots
long hair, cowboy hats.
'They came all the way from England,' Mum cried,
as she stroked their rugged features.

Now, almost forty years on.
The Diddy Men, discoloured
sit on the kitchen's Welsh dresser
I smile
remember.

masks

faces
content   sombre   furious
layers never end
take a deep breath
count to ten
then unpeel each one

tears from yesterday
smiles for tomorrow
ponder the now

depth   clarity
embrace change
unlock rooms of memory
snakes and ladders

search
question
pockets of discovery
subtle breeze whispers
through open window

Normal Day

Women wait
at the West Bank bus stop
eyes dart
lips quiver.

One chews her nails
another combs her hair
while the oldest of the three
fidgets with her headscarf.

From a car
rapid gun shots
screams slice morning air.

A bloodstained comb
slides into the gutter.

Resemblance

I saw another walker today.
The frail, wispy-haired figure
used it like my mother had,
not placing it firmly on the ground
before she stepped inside.
I wondered had she been in rehab long?
Was she still trying to cope?
Did she have a fall stroke?
Or was it an ear imbalance?
Did she impose unrealistic demands
on husband, daughter, son?
Needing their attention
no matter what.
But her fingers were devoid of rings.
I noticed her set mouth
as she banged the walker
along the footpath,
clinging to hope
perhaps threats of a nursing home
were ominously close.
She stopped banging her walker,
straightened her shoulders, lifted her chin,
then gave me a brief smile.

And for a moment
I saw my mother.

Looking Back

Dreams decay
       in
cobwebbed attic.
Lies smoulder
       in
shadows.
Child shivers
       in
damp cellar.
Gentle sobs
       in
bolted room.
Tap trickles tears
       in
bath of bones.
Wisteria whispers
       on
paint-flaked walls.
Horror haunts
       an
untamed garden.
Adult stumbles
closes eyes tight.
Sinks to haunches
shoulders shake.

The Outcast

Alone with her memories
hidden desires.
She closes eyes to escape
matriachal
black-clad figures
acid tongues
gold-toothed smiles.
Yearns
for guilt-free hours
grips wilting flowers
shivers at lengthening shadows
she remains trapped
in regrets
fears
lies.

CPSIA information can be obtained
at www.ICGtesting.com
Printed in the USA
LVHW021545040522
717862LV00014B/581

9 781761 093128